W9-CEN-015

Fears of Your Life
+ How FEARFUL CAN YOU BE?

also by
Michael Bernard Loggins

Imaginationally

Michael's Lovable Fun of
Dictionaries.

Fears of Your Life
+ How Fearful Can You Be?

Written and illustrated
by
Michael Bernard Loggins

WITH A NEW PREFACE BY
HARRELL FLETCHER

Manic D Press
San Francisco.

Copy right 2004, 2012 by
Michael Bernard Loggins
Published by Manic D Press.
All rights reserved. No Part
OF This book may be used or
reproduced in any manner whatsoever
without written Permission of the Publisher
except in the case of brief quotations
embodied in critical articles or reviews.
For information address Manic D Press,
P.O. Box 410804 San Francisco,
California 94141   ISBN 978-1-933149-61-5

Book Design by Jason whitlow.
Printed in Canada.

Part of "Fears of Your Life."
was Originally Produced as part
of the zine" Whipper snapper
Nerd" Published by Harrell Fletcher
and Elizabeth Meyer.

PREFACE

When I was in graduate school in the early 1990s my friend, Elizabeth Meyer, introduced me to Creativity Explored, an art studio for artists with developmental disabilities located in the Mission District of San Francisco. I'd never had any direct association with people who had "developmental disabilities" and was filled with uninformed assumptions and ideas about the limitations created by those curtailed abilities. Just entering into the studio at CE for the first time was a mind-blowing experience that quickly reset my understanding. The artists I encountered were talking to me, showing me their work, and offering me a bite of their sandwiches all at once. It was overwhelming but totally fascinating too, especially in comparison to the much less friendly and dynamic experience I was having at my school's grad studios. Michael Loggins wasn't around that first day, but I heard a lot about him and his work—he was sort of a star at the center even in those early days.

Over the next few years Elizabeth and I worked on various projects with the artists at CE. One of the things we did was to produce a photocopied magazine called *Whipper Snapper Nerd* (another artist at CE, John McKenzie, came up with the title). Each issue (we created eight in total) featured the work of one artist from CE along with a bio and interview. We decided to devote the first issue to Michael Loggins. His work was perfect for photocopying: it was often text-based, very graphic, and small scale enough that it didn't have to be reduced in size very much. At that point CE seemed to focus attention mostly on artists making big colorful work, so a lot of Michael's smaller text-based work was being stored away in boxes and flat files. Elizabeth and I started digging around in these mostly forgotten storage places looking for possible work for our magazine. At some point I ran across a pad of paper with text at the top in Michael's handwriting that said this: "Tuesday November 11 Month 17, Day 1992. Things that you are very Fearful of." Below that and on the following pages was a long numbered list that I started to read. By the time I had finished I knew that I had run across a masterpiece. I showed the list to Elizabeth, and soon after that, in consultation with Michael, we made a photocopied book version of the list with the title changed (by Michael) to *Fears of Your Life*. It was smallish with a bright red cover and was an instant hit; we had to make more and more copies of the publication to keep up with demand. Since that time, *Fears of Your Life* has been reproduced in *Harper's* magazine, exhibited in museums and galleries, was read on the NPR radio show *This American Life*, turned into a dance performance, and of course published as a book (by Manic D Press). I think that of all the projects I've been associated with in the last twenty years or so, Michael's *Fears of Your Life* has probably gotten the most mileage of any of them.

Michael is now a close and valued friend, and is also one of my favorite artists. His work in *Fears of Your Life* and beyond is amazingly complex, thoughtful, and emotionally perceptive. The hope that Elizabeth and I had when we started volunteering at CE was that by using zines and cable access videos we could help to make the work of CE artists available to a larger audience. It now gives me great satisfaction to continue to help spread the word on Michael Loggins and his incredible work.

Harrell Fletcher
11.2.11
Portland, Oregon

PART ONE

Things that you are very Fearful of

1. Fear of Hospitals and Needles.

2. Fear of School and Dentists.

3. Fear of Black Cats.

4. Fear of Monsters being under my bed. Fear of intruders coming into the house to steal things and hurt us all.

5. Fear of going to jail as being punish for doing something very wrong and have to stay in for a long time.

6. Fear of being followed.

7. Fear of Dogs.

8. Fear of Strangers.

9. Fear of time Bombs.

10. Fear of Deep waters.

11. Fear of Noises and bumps in the middle of the night.

12. Fear of being chase by bulls.

13. Fear of being Lost.

14. Fear of Elevators.

15. Fear of Doors when they Slams.

16. Fear of Fires and Smokes.

17. Fear of Guns and Knives.

18. Fear of Authority and Punishment.

19. Fear of Toys that comes on by itself without anyone touching it.

20. Fear of someone doing wrong to you and don't want you to do wrong back to them.

21. Fear of spiders and Roaches. and mouse raccoons and Rats too.

22. Fear of getting in deep trouble. or going to get in deep trouble.

23. Fear of being caught with another woman after Cheating on your wife.

24. Fear of getting run over by a car when not paying attention.

25. Fear of being caught by being with the person that steals.

26. Fear of Bees.

27. Fear of getting left alone.

28. Fear of going to the Doctor.

29. Fear of Riding in deserted Areas when it's dark.

30. Fear of your life being in great Danger and threaten.

31. There's Los Angeles Fears.

32. Oakland Fears.

33. San Francisco Fears.

34. Fear of torados and Thunders, and lightning too.

35. Fear of being in wrong Places at the wrong time.

36. Fear of dropping your Soda as it hit the ground and Fiz on You.

37. Fear of Planes.

38. Fear of insects.

39. Fear of television when you are afraid that it might Blow out all the lights in the house.

40. Fear of getting hit over the head when you carry lots of dough with you or Bucks.

41. Fear OF Getting in trouble by the Law. When you aren't going by rules.

42. Fear OF Death.

43. Fear OF Cemetery as you Drive by There at Night.

44. Fear of Tall Giraffe.

45. Fear of some birds.

46. Fear of Bears.

47. Fear that the television will Explode if you turn it on.

48. Fear of Earthquakes and Volcano's.

49. Fear of a blasted music on the Radio when you are not aware that the Volume is turn up.

50. Fear of being spankin by a Principal when a parent Give an permission.

51. Fear of Sexually Abused.

52. Fear of rolling down Hill Backward.

53. Fear of Bats.

54. Kids Feared that whatever they have done wrong that they afraid of getting Punishment or their Parents will kill them.

55. Fear of Heights.

56. Fear of storms.

57. Fear of being different.

58. Fear of getting shot.

59. Fear of getting put out the house.

60. Fear of if I do something naughty I will cause something to happen to me and I will get into trouble.

61. Fear of Rattlesnakes.

62. Fear of Fog Horn.

63. Fear of High tides.

64. Fear of Pirates.

65. Fear of Blackouts.

66. Fear of Disease and Germs.

67. Fear of Hurricanes.

68. Fear of witches and Gobblins.

69. Fear of Dangerous weApons.

70. Fear of Dragon.

71. Feared that if you get in the way of a Tall tree when it get chop or sawed For it to come tumbling Toward you get out of the way because it liable to Fall on you and Kill you and it wouldn't be Such a beautiful sight to See.

72. Fear oF Firecrackers and Cherry bombs. Fire works.

73. Feared wind and Rain Heavy Rain. Hailing Rain.

74. Fear oF Police.

75. Fear oF Scary Ghost Stories.

76. Fear of wild Animals.

77. Feared that you will get scald by a skillet on a stove if it turn over on you. if it get real Hot!

78. Fear of being barefooted walking around the House without any shoes on your Feet Just liable to get tuck on a tack or Glass or Nails or piece of Metal or Something.

79. Fear of Nightmare.

80. Fear of hurting themself.

81. Feared of being left in the house alone afraid that there would be an Earth quake in Few more Seconds.

82. Fear that if you are bad or naughty Noone's isn't going to Love you any more.

83. Fear of a Glass table if it cut you.

84. Fear of Dreaming that you have got sunk down into Quick sand.

85. Feared that if you put too much of toilet paper in the toilet Bowl it will run over and get all over the Floor and on you and on someone else too. It would leak From up stairs to the Next Floor Below.

86. Fear of somethings that are Scary.

87. Fear of getting hugged by somebody you don't like is Scary.

88. Fear of stepping down from something that is higher than you thought it was is scary.

89. Fear of Roller Skating down Hill when you haven't learned How to stop is Scary.

90. Fear of Doing something you shouldn't be doing is Scary.

91. Fear of something that you think that could be in the closet that might be scary is scary.

92. Fear of cars when they skid like if you think they're going To crash is scary.

93. Fear of Cows and Buffalo's

94. Fear of a dark house.

95. Fear of hearing somebody coming towards the door at Midnight.

96. Feared michael heard the Cable on the 5 Fulton Bus popped like a loud Firecracker it Scared him and the Bus driver Sunday November 11, 1992. At Midnight.

97. Fear Something is Scaring Blackie tonight.

98. People are fearful of me which I wonder is they think that I'm all that terrible or I'm thinking that they think I'm not Human at all Because when they sit next to me than they get back up and move away From me I maybe a stranger But that doesn't make me a Created monster or Something like that. People Aren't Humans they Act like Ignorance Dogs with their tail in back of their legs or in Between their middle Bodies their legs. they don't Think who's Feelings they hurt at all they Just do it No Consideration For whatever.

99. People don't think about how they hurt my feelings or don't give a hoot they don't give a crap.

100. Ignorance: No kind of sense at all whatsoever stupid and conceeded and no consideration for me always scared and move away to the next seat from me. People now a days are mean only thinking of themselves noone else.

101. What people think of
when they see me coming
up the street?
What the First thing
that they can think of
once they see a stranger
like me coming in the
Direction I goes in ?
Nothing But Fear!

102. why do people when they
see me coming what do
they tell their Friends?
let's cross the street I
don't want to get Hurt.

103. We better cross the
     Street this man is
     Following us and he wants
     To bother us what we
     ought to do is Turn and
     go another Direction
       Fear.

104. what does Fear itself can
     do to make you afraid of
     a stranger and what does
     that Fear tells you about
     that man And what Fear
     Cause you to think Something
     may happen to you in just
     5 Seconds or 1 minute?
     Does Fear warns people to
     move away From him or is
     it that it's a warning system
     tells you that man is ready For

104 continued on: An attack you and Harm you or what Kind of Danger your life is when you or guys and girls think To do is it lot threatening or Just a Kind of situation you may Face soon?

105. what is Fear? what does Fear tells you about a Stranger? Does Fear makes you clever or Does it warns you that you and your Friends Needs to Protect yourselves From Danger!

106. Does Fear makes you **Smart** or Does it Takes you over? It tries But it also save your life! It helps you To avoid Problems and Protect You and Keep you Safe From Harm.

107. I better not stick my Feet out in the Side of my bed or the monsters will bite me or wanting to eat me so I better stay Feet. That's Fear For you!!

108. People that say that they aren't afraid of anything is ashamed To admit it and they are Just Plain ignorance and just lying to admit that they have as much Fear as the next guy they Know

that they DO Fear Different things
they are lying Because they don't
want anyone to Know how Fearful
they really are.

109. mamma's fearful of michael's
little T.v. is that she's afraid
That it liable to blow out all
the lights in the house. But
I Solve her Fear by showing
her that it works pretty good
now I still don't Know if she
is Fearful or not? Are you?
yes or No circle which
Answer is what you choose
is right.

110. Fear of Ghost stories in the
Dark room.

111. Fear of Boogeyman.

112. Fear of Killer Bees.

113. Fear of Draculars.

114. Fear of werewolf.

115. Fear of mummy.

116. Fear of widow spider.

117. Fear of Haunted House.

118. Frankenstein is Fearful.

119. Dinosaurs is Fearful.

120. Fear of sharks.

121. Fear of Giantman.

122. Fear of Gorilla.

123. Fear of Godzilla.

124. Fear of Tall woman.

125. Fear of Killer whales.

126. Fear of Dinosaurs bird.

127. Fear of invisiable man.

128. Fear of Blob.

129. Fear of getting molester.

130. Fear of mountain lion.

131. Fear of Apes.

132. Feared when you don't Know that you Feel that somebody liable to sneak up on you as if you were being surprised. is scary.

133. Fear is like this: someone like a woman that you grab a hold of her hand and going down the escalator when of a sudden you happens to be holding a stranger hand not realizing that she isn't your mother is scary.

134. Fear is like this: If you are ever getting out of your car and not Alert and just going on doing what you normally wouldn't dreamed of doing, not paying Attention and not Thinking clearly or not Focusing on what is happening and not aware or not careful some how ended-up locking your Baby in a closeded in door to your car will have you Panic and it's scary.

135. Fear is like this: Bump in a person that is tall and slim and much older than You standing In line in front of you and you didn't know all that much about him at all you were in Back on him Playing or talking kind of light type tone voice and hetook at you with mean expression on his Face Saying are you talking to me oh No I were thinking about Something else. You feel scared Because you think that he thought you were mumbling to yourself in his presence which you thought that You were talking a stranger that isn't your Brother is scary.

136. Staying up late late late at night watching Horror movies alone is scary.

137. Feared that the Bus Driver
is Driving much Too Fast
like if He don't know How
to stop it or He tries
slowing it down some so
that he wouldn't Hurt up
Bunch of passengers.
They're scare of his
Driving.

138. Fear of Jumping off
the Bridge way up
High going down real deep
Splash in that Deepest
water and take your own
Life away From yourself.
You'll Jump From Top ledge.

Part II

---

what fears can do to you

Fear # 1.

If you run in the rain, you can slip on a wet pavement which is made out of cement

Equipment also stands For Ground as in Light Gray and Dark Gray as Michael Bernard Loggins Choose to Call Those Things:

Fear # 2.

I Fear that those tv.
People would take off
My Favorite cartoon.
the Rugrats OFF the Air
And Wouldn't be able to
WAtch Them Anymore For
a long long, long time.
"Please let Well enough alone".
Please Don't take my Rugrats
Cartoon off the Air Because
I Love that cartoon.
Let there Be a Possibility
that Life with the Rugrats
Stays Put Means Leave my
Rugrats Cartoon on tv. Michael said.

Fear # 3.

Want to Know more about
Fears: And what it can
happen to you if you
still be afraid and you
hasn't really truly over
Come the Kind of Fear
that you happens to have
on you? You look like
you'll almost never
get your chance of
over coming it like if
you are Home alone.

Fear # 4.

what will happen if
No one in this Life
inside their community
would ever get over their
Fears of over coming
The Fact that they're
really TErrifyed of
Scariest Movies and
Scariest Car Scares Crashes
or Scariest Halloween
Horroriest most Frightened
Holiday Seasonal christmas
Time events on T.V. Set.
in their Homes:

Fear # 5.

I'm afraid of my Fear of
Crossing the streets of
San Francisco when there
are so much safety rules
of streets For people to
go by the Laws and not
break those safety rules of
Those streets to those whom
Liable to be Playing Ball or
Cat and dogs and people may
be Crossing them may Be
Fearing that something aWFul
liable to happen to some of
Them.

Fear # 6.

Fear that if I go into the Library and I happens to get like 9 or 8 Books and I happens to Find a place in the Library that I would get a lot comfortable and Begin Reading in those 7 and 8 Books but one Book at a time and I Start to read and (Some How my Voice of mine start to get From low to High and thinking that there weren't anyone Elses) reading theirs and I Look over the people in the Library and I get Fearful and I'll say OOp's sorry.

Fear # 7.

Only Dangerous thing about
Stop Lights they don't Stay
on Long enough For you to
Change your mind about
Crossing the street. Look
Like it Should stay on
Like 45 seconds so that
you Can go Cross the
Street. But when they
Stay on For 30 seconds
They start to Change
Before you get to go across
the Street. Fear that
Someday those stoplights going
to get you Killed by lots of
Charging racing Cars Coming your
way And that wouldn't be such
a Pretty Sight to see If you
get my drift Sir.

Fear # 8.

One time when Michael Bernard Loggins went out by San Francisco Ocean Beach in California like real Late at Night while the Buses were still running, He saw this Raccoon Diggins in the Garbage can For Food to Eat Michael once Looked over at that Animal and Hurried over on the other side of the street by where the mountain is til He got Fearfully of that Animal and try to go as Far as He can til He's is out of that Raccoons Sight where the Raccoon can't see Michael anymore, Michael went for the Bus.

Fear # 9.

Fear of Being with a Friend
that you have recently met
start to take you Places with
him and you doesn't know him
all that well. You didn't know
that he were gonna bring
you Fear and lots of trouble
your way. Someone you doesn't
know all that well starts to
carry you in the store to buy
you and him something to Eat
and Drink and All of a sudden
something very fishy starts to
Happen: Like For instance
your Friend that you are with
could be up to trouble And
whoever with him could be
heading in For Trouble as well
especially if a Friend of yours
could be bringing you trouble by
stealing a big package of orero cookie.

Fear # 10

I Sometimes Fear that
when I walk down our
worses steepest Hill
on our street At olmstead
and Dartmouth I Fear
That some day My Knee
Joint liable to give out
And I wouldn't be able to
walk on my Leg til someone
In my Family rush me up
To the Hospital to Have an
Operation on my Knees
in order to get them to
Work once again, where
they can get back to
Walking all over again so
Michael Bernard Loggins
Feel ReFreshed and New Again.

Fear # 11.

Fear of Different kinds of Things.

1. Afraid to be in your bedroom alone.

2. Afraid there's a monster underneath your bed.

3. Afraid to be around Troublemaker People up to No good.

4. Going to Restaurants where you are afraid of People you doesn't know sitting around with a cup with change. And Decide that he wants your money and all of it.

5. what will you do if you were on your own what can you do if something happens would you Panic or Break out into BIG Fear.

Fear # 12.

Fear if you put things
that doesn't Belongs in
Your Ears And you Bust
The Drums thats are in
Your Ears it Liable to run
You deaf where you can't
Hear anything at all.
You wouldn't be able to Hear
Cars when they're Coming at
You. That can be a Frightening
and very Horrible situation
to Happen to you If it hada
Occurrance in real Life
especially if you comes
involved in it.
Can you get Hit by cars
if you can't Hear them.

Fear # 13.

Fear of troublemaker zone
starts with people starting
Trouble on Every single
Transportational like Cars
Buses - Trains - streets
-malls - and Banks and Parks.
They May Be all over the
Place.
Fear.
Feel AS Do if You are trap
inside a Fire of a High
UP Floor in a Highup Building
Some place in a room and
Can't get out. call the
Fire Department. It's in
Emergency. A woman or
a child or a Man - or a Boy
is in Some trouble, House on Fire.

Fear # 14

Would you be Fearful
if a rain cloud stodd
over your Head and rain
All over you?

Would you be Fearful if
It FolLows You Everywhere
you go And it just Scares
the Heck out of you?

The rain Clouds is so Dark
Gray Weather we have and
It start to Pour like lots of
Buckets of rain watér All
over You and You will be
All Drenched   all over
Yourself From The rain
Water itself said Michael
Bernard Loggins.

Fear # 15.

Going down the hills on a
wagon and Don't Know How
to stop it and Feel that
You are going to tip over
On your Body and your
Pretty Face And Be hurted
all over and Ache all over
Your whole body would be
a lot Fearfulliness.
And very scary too.

Fear # 16.

I was Fear of these two Dogs
That Man had with him when
He was out walking down on
Haight and Cole street yesterday
Michael Bernard Loggins has a
Bad case of Anixety and
He's Afraid of those two Pitt
Bulls except my own Dog
Blackie: I Love him said
Michael Bernard Loggins:

Pitt Bulls are very very
Dangerous to us ALL.

Fear # 17.

Have you ever get the
Feeling that if you
go out in the worser
wintertime bad weather
that you Fear that
you just liable to get
the worser wintertime
Cold And have to Stay
in bed lot longer than
you intended to do?
worser wintery cold
seasonal rest of
the wintertime in
your Bed in the
House.

Fear # 18.

When I went out by San
Francisco Ocean Beach of
Greathighway. These people
were sitting by this one
House when I got off the
71 Haight and Noriega Bus
To go toward My Brother Darryl
and My sister in-Law Simone
House Then These people two
Dogs Come towards Michael
Bernard Loggins like if they
want to Attack him. Just
because hE Happens to be
Let off The Bus on that side
of the street like if those
Dogs Feel like they own it.
Yes, Michael Bernard Loggins
Got Fearful and Scared
Thought those Dogs were gonna
Come After him or Chase him.

Fear # 19.

Fearful of using the Bus
that I normally would ride
going home or going for my
Outtings and These Bus Drivers
Drives Pretty Crazy and
Very Frightfully that you
have to Grabbs onto Bars
in order to Brace yourself
From Further Accidental
Crash or Tip the Bus Over
on it's Sides and You Liable
to get seriously hurt or Lucky
to come out of it Alive or
Die. Now that's the Possibility
that Life is an Sacrafice
that Life Challenge you:

Fear # 20.

I'm Afraid and Fearful
That Pigeons don't Know
Right From wrong to not go
out into the street.
They Don't have the kind of
Memory as we humans
does to know what to do
And what shalt Not Do.
They must Don't Know the
Danger of their Lives
are Being Jeopardize and
They Must Don't know
What can definitely
happen to them to Human's
Knowledges in sense,
Right Safe Lives and
Danger wrong Lives of theirs.
they Land just Any where
they can Find to Land on surface.

Fear # 21.

Michael is afraid and Frightening and Fearful when Andreascher goes away For a very very, very Long Long, Long, Long VACAtional Trips in order To go Traveling all over the world almost like different places and different Cities and countries to visit People in her own Image and Own Langaage. He Afraid Andrea scher would come back to San Francisco California with all Different Accents and won't be able to speak Michael's English or not be able to understand his words that he's telling her. Like Merry Christmas!

Fear # 22.

I am Afraid Someday I Liable to get lost inside Children's Hospital if I'm not all so familiar with that place yet. It's going to take some time to get use to it. Fearfully of that Great big Humungous Children's Hospital There ever would be to Michael's Knowledge. Good that Michael's Sister is Driving him up there on Tuesday January 15, 2002. even though she's with him she Can easily get lost too.

Bad situation to tangled up in. especially if you that Person has an Appointment at 10:45 Am in The morning. Michael Bernard Loggins does.

Fear # 23.

Francis-Michael is Afraid to
To tell you that Christmas
Day is gonna be on a
Wednesday December 25,
2002 this coming year.
And tuesday December 24,
 2002 will be totally Different
Than Before. It won't be
Just like Before. I think
Wintertime will be on Sunday
December 22, 2002 winter
Seasonal Year that We'll be
having and happens to have.
all at once in a Lifetime
Guaranteed at your bargain
Price just one of michael's
Wintertime humority Funny
Word to Describe his Funny
Humorous Joke Just For the
Laughs of Laughter. by Michael
Bernard Loggins. Keep us Laughing.

Fear#24

Michael is afraid and very
Frightening and Fearful to
Talk all day And Not get
any work done in order
to get some money But
Michael Fear if He Joke around
Too much and doesn't do his
work he wouldn't get any
money at all.
If he Fool around and not
get his work catch up on.

oh! my goodness
is Michael
Really seriously
afraid of that?

Fear # 25.

Fear of People Popping Fire Crackers and Any kind of Dangerous Fire Chemical Gun Powder around where Cars are Parked - People Frightens michael Bernard Loggins where he Sits at especially be where Cars are Parked - People Could Put Michael Bernard Loggins Life in danger Just being too carelessness of the Situation and Don't have No Care in the world what So ever if They Act as if They don't have Senses of 5 Just the way God Gave us to have to use. If in Case 4th of July ever Comes back I Just Hope it don't be trouble at all.

Fear # 26.

Fear your Life is really a challenge and a Possibility and choice and serious Danger and warning: and Sacrafice to Pick: There's Trouble out into the streets of San Francisco California With These Crazier People Driving Behind these Wheels Of these Automobiles hurting and Hitting People is very Frightening And very nerve Wreckins to your Safety and Life too.

Fear # 27.

Michael Fear that if his teacher Francis Doesn't Put away Michael's Top Ramen Noodles up in The Desk Drawer that Douglas will see it and He'll Liable to want to take it and He'll happens to Eat up Michael Bernard Loggins' Noodles himself And Michael Bernard Loggins would be out of Luck But He would Have to go Home tonight and Bring Back to school another Pack of Noodles to Eat Himself So that Wouldn't Ever Ever Happened With that Douglas Eat up Noodle Story.

Fear # 28.

It's very scary and
Fearfully to be sleeping
in Your Bed in the middle
of the Night whenever
There's a Telephone
right beside the bed
on your Left Near the
Door you once Enter and
Exit out. You are sleeping
The Telephone rang and
scare the Living Life out
of you, in the middle of the
Night. "Who is this calling
at this Hour of Night?

Fear # 29.

I would be Afraid if a car
Somewhere Almost close.
And it was going to Explode
I would run as Fast as I
can to get out of the way
of it so That I wouldn't
get Hurt by it. I'll get away
as Far as I can or Hit the
Deck Means to Drop Down
and wish it don't get you
It's a car Exploding, It's a
Scary Situation For you
to see would it ever occur
For Real or does it Happen
So Other or What Happens
after a car are through Exploding
will The Fire Fighters Puts The Fire out?

Fear # 30.

There's a possibility
That something fearful
and very Scary
Liable to Happen
which is a warning
sign that you can't
Understand what it
means can Scare the
Heck out of you.

Fear # 31

Watch a Fearful Movie at Night
Late and when you go to bed
to sleep then All of a sudden
The Nightmare start to
Happen And You start to
Break a sweat From having
an Anxiety Depression
Scariness and FearfulNight-
Mare Pictures in your Mind.

Nightmare is a Dream
that frightens People.

Freddie Kruger Don't exist
in the realLife, The world
only in Movies - Nightmare
on Elm street. The Fiction
Stories on But Never REAL
                    LiFE.

Fear # 32.

Fear of People up to No
Good Making Trouble in
our Community and
Schools and in our

Neighborhoods And our
cities too;

" streets of Trouble
maker Hood."

Fear # 33.

Fear of you Never known you
were gonna lose your Mother
is very Sad and Scary
Experience you have to Face
and learn From and you
wonder why she has to die
I Love her- And I had Loved
her once while she were Alive.
especially if she was the
Mother that raised you and
the others through Birth
And you only wish that you could
have done all you can to Help
Save her Life.

It Gonna be a worse times
and hard times For Michael
Bernard Loggins and his
Sisters and Brothers too.
especially when Mother's Day comes.

Fear # 34.

If your friends are people
that you are with and you
Hear them making Decision
about what they DEcide That
they are gonna steal expensive
and very valuable Merchandise
out of the Department stores
and don't careless. You Say I'm
out of hEre! Bye-bye. I'm not
getting caught in your crazy
schemes. I'm Not your stealer
partner, Im just your Friend.
it's gonna trouble And it's on your
head not mine. I'm not gonna
Participate in stealing with
you. So Leave me out out of
Your crazy schemes especially
If it involves oreo cookies
and other stuff. Hot stuff.
Fear of me getting In trouble
Just as well.

Fear # 35

I Fear that in the story
of Little Red riding Hood the
Girl goes out in the woods
by herself (without Anyone
else going too)to her Grandmothers House so that she
wouldn't Just get suspicious
that something Liable to
Happen to the Girl all in
the woods alone trying to
get to her Grandmothers
House And Delivers a Basket
of Goodies to her Grand-
mother and what happen
is that her Grandmother
turns out to be the Mean and
worser wolf around- want to
Eat up the Girl it's ownself.

Fear # 36.

Life can be very challege.
When it comes to Danger
and Crossing the streets of
San Francisco and other Streets
And Other parts of the world
especially in other Neighborhoods
Is where Fear Lurkes out For
You in Some way.
Bring you lots of Fears and
Trauma in your Hands Feets
and Body.
Bring you shakes and Trembles
To you.

Fear # 37.

Grabbing onto Someone elses
Grandmother which you thought
She were yours And you
haven't ever thought that
Those Grandmother's that
You haven't seen that has
Passaway From what your
Parents has told you that
Your Grandparents Has
Passaway Before you were
Born is Scary and Fearful
Situation to be in.
Yes. it Can Happen by
Accident.

Fear # 38

Walking into a lion's cage and petting it on the head can be a Ticklish situation, and not in a funny way.

Fear # 39.

I would be very Fearful If I Reached up on top shelf Trying to Reach For a Nice Thicker Covered Dictionary Book And Not ask for Help From Someone and the Books Come OFF the shelf and Make lots of noises and the People gets Angry at me and Don't understand that I had want Help But I were Afraid to ask For it and they be a Jerk or a Creep as Hope tells me and People Say that I'll have to Pay For the Shelf and I get in lots of Trouble behind it. Says Michael.

Fear # 40.

Fear of streets in our
Cities and communities
and Neighborhoods are
very rare sometimes
People are very carelessly
designated drivers unImpatience
Not Given you any time whatsoever
Crossing the streets of San Franc
isco, Making it or Cities in the
world a lot unsafe For children
Adults and Animals to Cross Them
and Makes us Paralyzed From
the waist on down to your Feet.
How dangerous streets really
are these days in our Lives:

Fear # 41.

Michael Bernard Loggins hae to Move the Noodle Bowl with the Noodles in it over So he wouldn't knock it off the table and Bust the Bowl open into Pieces And Noodles all over the Creativity Explored center Floor, I Feared it Liable to Happen that way. So that's why I Kinda Shoved the Bowl over in the Middle of my table to Prevent it From Happening to it Breaking to Pieces or in Half too.

Fear#42.

I Fear that when I'm
going across the street
on Folsom and 16th I
FEAR that these people
in these cars is going to
Seriously hurt me or
really take my Life
For sure definitely
The way they act
Foolishly and Very
Dangerously with their
Bad worsest Driving
Uneducational Skill
Don't Need Any License to
Be Handled any vEhicles.

Fear # 43

Fear And Traumatized
Frightful Experience of
Your Life Michael
Bernard Loggins Books
He was making as All
Stories that He invented
on his own in his head.
Thoughts coming out
like left and right.
Didn't Know How Fast they
was coming at me., It's
like Somebody were get
ready to throw a Fast
Ball at the Base Ball Game.
Says Michael Bernard Loggins.

Fear # 44.

Two   Fear of my hand is
Hurting and why is it
Hurting when I'm writing
according on how hard I'm
Holding my Pen And If it
keep on Hurting it liable
to Hurt a lot worser
Than Now. Says "michael
Bernard Loggins."

Fear # 45

Afraid this is the Last
Thing that ever occur
to me. this is the End
of Fears of your Life
Page in my Book.
Tuesday February 19,
2002. is when michael
Bernard Loggins Finishes
These Pages UP. so there
be the Last to be done.
For michael Bernard
Loggins. Congradulation!
michael My Buddy Buddy!
Pal you Did it you got it done.

HOW FEARFUL CAN YOU BE?
by MICHAEL BERNARD LOGGINS.

This is A DEDicated Gift
This Book is For my
Girlfriend in my Life
Every since August 2,
1991 - And Here we're in
August 2009. To
HopeGoodall I Truly
Dedicate my Love to you
Personally, It's Almost
Feels as Though I'm Giving
You Actual Christmas
Present to the one that are
Closed at my middle of my
     Heart.

Life can really be scary
Sometimes very creepy
Feeling to have as Though
You have saw a Monster
Comes up From the top
of the ocean - About to
Come on Land - Run
For Your Life.

You Feel so tense up about
Seeing a creature Come
up From the ocean Floor
on to the Island to
ComFront you Face
to Face.

MR
Wide
Eyes
Exciter.

Fear of
being
Called
MR
Smiling
Too
much!
For
me
up
on
The
stage
in Life

Rozzy Barker Duck.

Fear of
War
What
War?
The
war
of herd of
Bats.

GLadys Danger Wind.

She
Fear of
her
Life
being
Call Danger
Wind Whirling

Pool
in the
wind.

ALLELi mae windson.

She
Love
her
Dad
But
Not
in Public
spot of
Life!

Fear she'd
be her
Daddy's
Favorite
Child
through
out her
LiFE.

Fear of being MR wide Water Guy

MR Water Field winston

Fear of
Being
Actually
Sliced
into a
Bigger
Piece of
Pie. How
Greedy!

MR
Halloween
John
Link

Friday zizzybelli

Fear of her Name Actually Represents Friday as beGinning of a weekend

Fear of
Shaking
in my
Boots
when
Facing
her in a
Dark Alley
when I go
Home.
Not so bright.

Mad
mammea
Yansberry
Hood.

Fear
of her
getting
a smile
in the
mirror
And Break
the mirror
in a Billion
pieces.

MRS weird
Scappy
Johnston

Lisa CaLA Basey

She's
afraid
of
Fearful
Insects
That
Appears
in her
Bedroom
when
She
Plays
her
Record
Player.

Rozen Candy Guy.

Fear of Coming back From the Store with a Protein Plus Candy Bar because it Liable to be taking away From me.

Big Poke out
Lip Skipper.

He Fear of
being Teased.
keep smile
Or Laugh
a smile
a Little
not be Pokey.

Betty Weather Bird.

Fear
Of
her
Name
Represents
Of her
Actually
Flying Free
Through
The
Air.

Bird
Of
Weather
Flyer
her
Appear-
ance.

Fear
of being
Called
Hey!
Kids
what's
New
MR
Light
Bulb?
Let me
turn you
on.

MR Bulb
Lenox
BLUER.

He is scare
SiLLy
HYSTerical
Smileness

Max Skipper LUANO.

Fear of
Eating an
Onion
get a
Hot taste

Fear of
Letter Hot
Hot, Food.

MR Jackerson SmuGG Dale

He Fearful
of the
DoGs
and Cats
and Allergic
To Crab
Sealion.
as well.
But he isn't
afraid watch
ing T.v.
News.

Mean mama ADora.

Fear of
Getting
up in
her Face
To talk
lots of
smack
And get smacked!

MR
Holloway
Fear of
being slick
moving on
STage Because
Of his Legs.

MR Hollow
Way Slick
Mover.

The Big
Knees
Suzie
beth.

Suzie is Fear
of going out in
public with such
Shorter Skirt
During the wind.

Fear
of
Facing
a
Monster
Through
a
Mirror
Each
morning
Of
my
Life!

The
Frankenstein
Boy

He don't
Look as
himself
Anymore!

Carl Watson Bridge.

He is Fearful of being on the corner of Fewer Street where People comes up to him trying to Sell Drugs and [illegible]. Alcohol and Coke. He not Apply to any of those Stuff.

Lisa weatherdance.

She is afraid
of being
Too sick
And she is
Fearful of
What Life
Throws onto
her Path.

Michael
Nicklson
Moneyson.

He Fears of
Having money
at his side
but Love Life.

Elizabeth Gate Waters.

Elizabeth is very Loved by her Family But she is Fearful of the Outside LiFE. that's all She's only Fearful of.

John Mattew Baker

He not
fearful
of
Busrides
But he
is Fearful
of Life on
the out-
side
World.
But he
Love to
be Loved.

He fear of mean And Danger-
ous DoGs that are in his
Neighbor-
Hood.

Ken
Juan
Ocean
Denver.

Ryan
Carlo
Black

What
are
you
Fearful
of Kid?

He's fearful
of
Roller coaster
Rides.

Fear
of
Working
at
Sears
Roe
buck
because
He don't
want to be
Seen on the
Top Floor

Marty
Seary
Teasley
Boyberry

Fear of
Bopping
a
Guy
Cross
the
Head
by
Teasing
Him
by his
Name

The
Fearful
monster
of the
Morning
Run
For
your
Life!
Not to
Love her.

Monster

Monster Lady.

MR Small Body Duffy.

Fear
of
having
People
Call
Him
Carton
body.
Duffy.

Lisa sally Green Bird.

Less
Fearful
of the
Un Known
to be
Fear of
Too much
Life in
Real world.

should
be very
Fearful
not
Less
Fear.
ful
Please!

October Reddy ZEN-Berg.

Fear of being not so trying hard to be Humor

Auto Lu bank.

Auto Lu bank
is fearful of
CLasaphobia
of Different
things that
Involves
Life.

Webster House Brooke.

him to have a Awful Nose bleed.

He get much too Sweaty at night Til He Can't Stand it.

Webster is fearful of the Summer Heat because He Can get his Fever and the Sun Cause

Trent Love Mattew.

Trent Feel he Should be Treat Fairly and be Loved as Well.

Trent is Fearful of being Mistreated unfair Just because Other Part of his brother John is Treated like a King.

Gate Benson trent.
Weird of being punish by that Name.

Gate Benson trent is Fearful Of being Send home Into his room to be Punished For Having Such a Name But Unfairly Judged Poorly Just Because of having a name Gate.

She's So Smiley Now, Until Night.

Patti
Cake
Jingles
is
Fearful
of
Flies
when she
have her
mouth wide
open at
Night!

MR Bellington is Fearful
of Horrible Nightmares.

Johnston
Ned
Bellington.

Honey Appleton Cender.

Fear of being Called Smiley Apple seed.

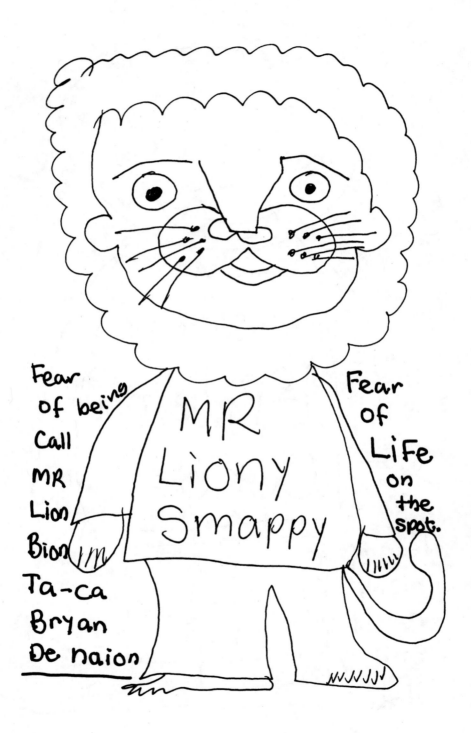

Fear
of being
Call
MR
Lion,
Bion
Ta-ca
Bryan
De naion

MR
Liony
Smappy

Fear
of
Life
on
the
spot.

Michael ZOO WELL Dish. The First:

Fear of Having to wash his own Dish Because

of his Last Name Call WELL Dish

MR Hot Fried zack.

FEAR
He
Only
Would
be
Mist-
aken as
a
Recipie
Fried
Sausage

Fear of
Being
Caught
in
the
Middle
of a
Hot
Sizzle
Sun!

Ralph
Blue
Bird
House
nick.

He Fear
of being
Called
Blue
Bird
in the
nest
House.

Tanerahh Taucer BLuey.

Fear of being called
So MR show off.

Januah Jerry scott.

Fear of
being
what
he calls
Appears
to be
really a
Fearful scary
Boy Nervous.

Lisa
Betsy
Lorrie
towel

Lisa
is Fearful
that some-
one that
doesn't
Like her
may tell
her Get
a Dry
Towel
to Put
over her
Head And soak.

Carl sea wiserman.

nothing
Wrong
With
this
man's
Name
That Just
What his
Name
is Given
to him
nothing
Personal
nothing to
tease him
aBout.

Carl
is
Fearful
of
being
Teased
by being
Call
sea
For his
middle
Name
because
he FeEL
that there
isn't wrong

He
Love
to
be
Call
max
Boylen.
too
Bad
Max
Heaven

Max
Heaven
Boylen
is suppose
to love
the Name
his Family
or Michael
Loggins
Gives him.
He Not so Loved.

Gaterson
Moven
Trats.

New Name
For a Famous
Guy. MR
Trats.
is
Fearful
of being
Call rats
Buns.
But his
Name is
Trats.
not rats.

Fear of being on the spot in Not Cute Section!

Skippey Roenberg Johnston.

Friday Wine Hart.

He Fear
Of being
Friday Season
Weather Base-
Ball Party Pooper

Yanzy Salt Mossizz.

Fear of
Having
Such a
Bigger
Head
For
a square
Neck
Kind of
Character
Guy.

ALLey Mae Lizzibeth.

Fear
of
Not
Wanting
To be
Fearful
Any
Longer.

Michael Bernard Loggins was born in 1961 in San Francisco, California.

He has been writing, drawing and painting at Creativity Explored since it's inception in 1984. His words and Art have been exhibited at galleries in San Francisco, Los Angeles and New York.

Michael has a sizable collection of 45's (somewhere in the neighborhood of 500-600 discs) and sings on occasion. He has a cassette tape of songs he has sung while accompanying himself on the coffee can.

His list of Fears have been enjoyed by a growing list of admirers and have been exhibited at the Yerba Buena Center For the Arts, Published in the Sun and Harper' Magazine, and read on NPR's This American Life.

Currently michael is most interesting in writing and this usually takes the Form of notes to Friends, issues on his mind (safety, allergies, emotions etc.) and recounting incidents From his Life. His Drawings generally deal with lighter subject matter such as animals, Idyllic Worlds and Imaginary People.

He likes spending time at Ocean Beach and the PanHandle near Golden Gate Park in San Francisco. He Frequently takes himself out to lunch and enjoys hangout at his girlFriend Hope's House till 8:30 P.M.

"THE thank you Note to people that I know in my Life. throughout my Life." "That's the titled."

1. I want to thank Francis For helping me with my Fears of Your life Book by helping me to get it Finish and ready to have it Published and ready to Be made. Michael and Francis Are doing the work together.

2. I want to thank my Girlfriend Hope Goodall For being my Girlfriend All the way up to 12 Years of being together in a long 12 years relationship with me And Say that You Love me a whole lot and I Love you too. and you go places with me and You treat me to Lunch Just the way I treated you Hope Darling Baby. You are my Love in this 12 year Relationship. From Friday August 2, 1991 you are the best.

3. thank you Erika Lee Altman and Katie Wyatt For Coming to creativity Explored Center 2 Art day Program to visit me and Hangout with me and most of all thank you both For taking me out to Lunch on You Guys spare time because we haven't got that Chance to do that in our lives till yesterday which was Thursday August 14th 2003. of a Hot and Breezy summertime Mix weather we Are having in August 2003. I want to thank my Mother For Everything you done.

4. thank you Todd For taking me out Places with you and Francis whenever I asked youguys Nicely. And sorry I didn't get a way of Crossing The Street of Mission and 16th on wednesday August 13, 2003. And I couldn't get a chance to Catch up to you and Francis by the time you botha got on the 49 mission and City College bus wednesday And the worse Part way I couldn't CatCh up to you and Francis at all. Not only that: My Foot start to hurt me real badly And I was in pain For a little While And I have came From Walgeens and Rode this other 49, mission and City College Bus And still I couldn't Catch up to you Guys For Nothing in the world! And the only thing that happened to me is on Vanness and Market street the Bus Driver on the 71 Haight and Noriega Bus took off and left me behind him and didn't give me Any time to get on the Bus And that's when I got Furious at him. He was too Impatient didn't have time to Wait for me what so ever. So my Foot begin to Hurt me instead.
Says Michael Bernard Loggins, I went straight To Jack's Record cellar.

creativity explored
WHERE ART CHANGES LIVES

Creativity Explored is a visual arts center in San Francisco where artists with developmental disabilities have been creating and selling art for over twenty years. To learn more about us, visit WWW. creativity Explored. org.

Life will be at Creativity Explored no matter what the circumstances will be.
Whether it's good - bad - or worse than what it seems or even those things Kind of get wacky, or slightly out of hand, soon or Later, These things blows over and return to what they will be.

- Michael Bernard Loggins.